Social Media and Financial Market Predictions

Table of Contents

1. Introduction 2

2. The Rise of Social Media: A Dynamic Shift 3

    2.1. The Genesis of Social Media 3

    2.2. The Social Media Avalanche 3

    2.3. Economic Implications and the Financial Market 4

    2.4. The Emotional Barometer: Social Sentiment Analysis 4

    2.5. The Crypto-Craze: A Case in Point 5

3. Soaring Tweets, Swinging Stocks: Understanding the
Connection 6

    3.1. The Power of Tweets 6

    3.2. Market Reaction: A Symbiotic Relation 7

    3.3. The Tweet-Stock Market Model: An Insight 7

    3.4. Parsing Tweets: Sentiment Analysis 8

    3.5. GOSSIPS - A Market Mood Tracker 8

4. Big Data and Social Sentiment: Measuring the Pulse of the
Market 10

    4.1. The Intersection of Big Data and Financial Markets 10

    4.2. Data Classification: Structured and Unstructured 11

    4.3. The Social Sentiment Analysis 11

    4.4. From Pulse to Prediction: The Role of Pattern Recognition ... 12

    4.5. The Power and Pitfall of Social Sentiment Analysis 12

5. Algorithmic Trading: The Social Media Fuel 14

    5.1. Why Algorithms? 14

    5.2. Social Media: The New Data Source 15

    5.3. From Text to Trading Signal 15

    5.4. Pitfalls and Contingencies 16

    5.5. The Future: Social Media-Fueled Algorithmic Trading 16

6. Machine Learning: The Brain Behind Successful Predictions 18

6.1. Machine Learning: An Overview 18

6.2. Finance & Social Media Data 18

6.3. Machine Learning at Play 19

6.4. From Data to Predictions: The Machine Learning Process . . . 19

6.5. The Way Ahead 20

7. Case Studies: The History of Market Movements Influenced by
Social Media 21

7.1. The Manic Monday of Facebook's Plummeting Stock 21

7.2. The Short Squeeze Saga: GameStop and Reddit's
WallStreetBets 22

7.3. Elon Musk's Tweets and Tesla Stock Volatility 22

7.4. Crypto-craze: Bitcoin, Dogecoin and Social Media Buzz 23

8. The Legal Landscape: Ethics, Privacy and Regulation 24

8.1. The Regulatory Framework 24

8.2. Privacy Concerns 24

8.3. Ethical Considerations 25

8.4. Navigating the Terrain 25

9. Modern Investor: Adapting to a Socially-Informed Market 27

9.1. Harnessing the Power of Social Media 27

9.2. Understanding Big Data 28

9.3. Grasping Social Sentiment 28

9.4. Leveraging Algorithmic Trading 28

9.5. Navigating the Legal Landscape 29

9.6. Practical Case Studies 29

10. Forecasting the Future: Predictive Trends and Models 30

10.1. Big Data and Predictive Modeling 30

10.2. The Invincibles: Machine Learning Predictive Models 31

10.3. Real World Model Implementations 31

10.4. Predictions: A Combination of Art and Science 32

10.5. Ethical Considerations and Regulatory Challenges 32

10.6. The Road Ahead 32

11. Social Media Investing: The New Norm and Best Practices 34

11.1. The Underpinnings of Social Media Investing 34

11.2. Best Practices for Social Media Investing 35

11.3. The Implications and Future Trends of Social Media Investing 36

In the future, financial markets could be all machine-to-machine, with humans at the periphery, creating algorithms.

Chapter 1. Introduction

In a world where social media's influence is rapidly permeating every facet of our lives, understanding its impact on financial markets has become more vital than ever. Our Special Report, 'Social Media and Financial Market Predictions' demystifies this phenomenon in an engaging, yet comprehensive manner. We traverse the complex terrain of big data, machine learning, and algorithmic trading, yet keep our narrative approachable, ensuring you don't need a Finance PhD to follow along. By unraveling the intricate ties between tweets, hashtags, and your stock portfolio, we aim to equip you with strategic insights that could potentially change your investment gameplan. With our Special Report, dive in to explore the exciting crossroads where finance meets social media, and discover unprecedented ways to leverage these digital trends for market predictions. Make an informed decision whether to buy, sell, or hold - all by keeping an eye on your social media feed!

Chapter 2. The Rise of Social Media: A Dynamic Shift

The Internet revolution has fundamentally altered our perception of the world by weaving an intricate lattice of global connectivity. Within this constantly evolving tapestry, a shift of monumental proportions has unfurled upon us, spearheaded by the phenomenon we refer to as social media. This chapter dives into an elaborate exploration of social media's indefatigable ascent, throwing light on how this digital marvel has reshaped our lives, societal structures, and ultimately, the financial markets.

2.1. The Genesis of Social Media

It is impossible to talk about the rise of social media without harking back to the early days of the Internet, a source of profound disruption in how we communicate, consume, and even exist. It was in this fertile soil of burgeoning interconnectivity that the seeds of social media were sowed. Websites like SixDegrees, an early pioneer in the field, and later, Friendster, and Myspace, aimed to replicate offline relationships in an online realm, fostering a sense of community amidst the sprawling expanse of the Internet. However, it was the advent of Facebook in 2004 that truly signalled the onset of the social media revolution, soon followed by Twitter in 2006, making social interaction and information exchange a mouse-click away. Today, platforms like Instagram, Snapchat, LinkedIn, and YouTube among others, have diversified this space, further propelling social media to new heights of ubiquity and influence.

2.2. The Social Media Avalanche

From a modest inception to its current standing as a critical fixture in our daily lives, the evolution of social media is akin to an avalanche—rapid, overpowering, and all-encompassing. Over 4.2 billion people around the world, more than half the global population, are active social media users today, spending on average nearly 2.5 hours daily on these platforms. Current projections suggest that by 2025, active social media users will cross the staggering 4.8 billion mark, cementing it as a fundamental facet of modern living. These figures underscore, quite emphatically, the mammoth impact of social media on our world, setting the stage for its meteoric influence on financial markets.

2.3. Economic Implications and the Financial Market

As social media platforms grew in number and versatility, so did their implications for the global economy. Platforms like LinkedIn revolutionized recruitment, giving rise to an employer-employee marketplace never seen before. Facebook and Instagram emerged as powerful platforms for businesses, small and large, to advertise, sell, and engage with their audience. Increasingly, even governments and institutions have realized the merits of communication via these channels, enabling more direct and fluid contact with their constituents and stakeholders. With time, the financial world, too, began to feel the tremors of this dynamic shift. Investors, traders, and analysts, traditionally reliant on earnings reports, financial news, and economic indicators, suddenly had an avalanche of 'real-time' data at their disposal, ripe for deriving insights about market sentiments, trends, and predictions.

2.4. The Emotional Barometer: Social Sentiment Analysis

The true power of social media in the financial realm, however, stems from its role as an emotional barometer of the masses. Social sentiment, or the collective mood and opinion of people extracted from their social media activities, has proven to be an immensely valuable tool for financial market predictions. With algorithms capable of tapping into this wealth of public sentiment, investors can glean critical insights, often ahead of traditional financial indicators, providing them a competitive edge in the volatile world of stock trading. This sentiment analysis, coupled with the instantaneous nature of social media, has the potential to influence trade decisions and investment strategies in unprecedented ways.

2.5. The Crypto-Craze: A Case in Point

A telling testament to social media's influence on financial markets is the recent crypto-craze. Tweets from prominent figures like Elon Musk have frequently set off tsunamis in the crypto-market, leading to significant shifts in the prices of cryptocurrencies like Bitcoin and Dogecoin. The sheer power of a single tweet, choppy or stabilizing, is a harrowing reminder of the new age we've entered, where social media's omnipresent role imprints its indelible marks on the charts of the financial market.

In conclusion, the rise of social media has not just been a dynamic shift, but a veritable paradigm shift, tearing down old barriers and enabling new connections. Its influence on the financial market, though still a topic of extensive research and debate, is undeniable. As we continue to dissect this fascinating intersection of technology and finance in subsequent chapters, we invite you to explore this evolving landscape, and perhaps, rethink your investment strategies in this socially-driven market.

Chapter 3. Soaring Tweets, Swinging Stocks: Understanding the Connection

In the fast-paced digital world, the connectivity between seemingly divergent elements can be surprisingly strong and consequential. One key domain of interest happens to be the intertwining narratives of social media chatter - particularly manifested in Twitter posts, or tweets, - and stock market fluctuations. This chapter endeavors to facilitate an enriched comprehension of this nexus to the reader.

3.1. The Power of Tweets

The advent of Twitter, an online social networking service where users post and interact through messages known as 'tweets, ' has revolutionized the way information is disseminated and opinions are aired. Within 280 characters, individuals are able to convey major sentiments around topical issues, and thus trigger considerable impacts on various spheres, including the world of finance.

In this interconnected ecosystem, a tweet doesn't merely represent an individual's perspective or recount the day's engagements. It has evolved into a tool that could potentially trigger market shifts and sway investors' decisions. For instance, Elon Musk's tweet stating "Am considering taking Tesla private at $420. Funding secured" sent seismic shocks through Wall Street, causing Tesla's stock price to surge dramatically.

3.2. Market Reaction: A Symbiotic Relation

This phenomenon of market movements paralleling social media discourse didn't take place in a vacuum. It arose from a complex, symbiotic relationship between market sentiment, trader behaviors, and digital chatter. In essence, soaring tweets can correspond to swinging stocks – either fueling escalating market enthusiasm, exacerbating market downturns or signaling a major shift in market sentiment.

The encapsulation of public sentiment within tweets can be employed as an indicator of the collective market mood. A slew of negative tweets surrounding a certain stock could potentially instigate a market sell-off, whereas a stream of positive tweets regarding a company could usher a purchasing wave.

3.3. The Tweet-Stock Market Model: An Insight

Quantifying this relationship warrants a more rigorous and systematic approach - a mathematical model that measures the correlation between the frequency and sentiment of tweets and stock market behaviors.

This model, dubbed as the 'tweet-stock market model,' forms an integral part of today's investment landscape. It looks at a vast array of data points such as the overall volume of tweets, positive or negative sentiment derived from these tweets, and key trigger words used surrounding a particular stock or the market as a whole. The interplay of these factors can be instrumental in shaping stock market movements.

Through this model, the impact of social media on the financial market becomes quantifiable, allowing for a more accurate representation of the market sentiment. For instance, if there is a marked increase in negative Twitter sentiment surrounding a company or sector, the model would predict a corresponding dip in the stock prices.

3.4. Parsing Tweets: Sentiment Analysis

To operationalize the tweet-stock market model, we deploy a technique called sentiment analysis or opinion mining. This involves the use of natural language processing, text analysis, and computational linguistics to discern and extract subjective information from source materials, a critical aspect in understanding social-media induced moods.

Segmenting tweets about stocks into 'bullish' or 'bearish' categories, sentiment analysis enables the conversion of abstract sentiments into measurable data. It extends beyond just the cursory reading of tweets, capturing nuances and implicit meanings that can provide valuable insights into public sentiment.

3.5. GOSSIPS - A Market Mood Tracker

Among various applications, Georgetown's Online Social-Sentiment-Index-Powered Securities (GOSSIPS) is a noteworthy tool. It adopts a unique sentiment-analysis-based model wherein each tweet about S&P 500 companies is broken down, analyzed, and aggregated into an overall score. GOSSIPS, through tracking the mood of the market via Twitter, transforms seemingly chaotic online chatter into a gauge of market sentiment.

In conclusion, tweets and stocks have a symbiotic relationship that is becoming increasingly significant for investors and market experts. The rise of sentiment analysis and advanced mathematical models has enabled a new form of market prediction and understanding. The impact of the Twitter conversation on the financial landscape is profound, reminding us that the pulse of the market now beats to the rhythm of the tweet.

Chapter 4. Big Data and Social Sentiment: Measuring the Pulse of the Market

The rapid digitalization of our lives has led to an ocean of data that we collectively refer to as Big Data. The advent of social media just turned the tap on, dramatically increasing the speed and volume of data generation. A quick glance at some numbers will suffice: every single day, we generate 2.5 quintillion bytes of data! A staggering 90% of the data in the world today has been created in just the last two years. From posts, tweets, shares and likes to photos, videos, blogs, and reviews, this digital pump is continuously gushing data in all shapes and sizes.

4.1. The Intersection of Big Data and Financial Markets

Analogous to a mega telescope lens that allows us to peer deep into the cosmos, Big Data grants us an unprecedented perspective of the complex world of financial markets. Traditional financial market models adhere staunchly to economic theories and numeric data – the hard facts such as revenue reports, GDP, inflation, and unemployment rates. But today's globalized and integrated world is too dynamic for such static models.

Big Data, on the other hand, welcomes markets' inherent dynamism by analyzing high volume, high velocity, and high variety data. From seemingly unrelated events like a controversial celebrity tweet to objective market data, everything becomes fodder for Big Data analytics - giving us a holistic, real-time understanding of market sentiments.

4.2. Data Classification: Structured and Unstructured

Technically, data often exists in two forms - Structured and Unstructured. While the former refers to identifiable patterns like spreadsheets, databases, etc., the latter is more chaotic, bearing no definitive pattern. It includes texts, tweets, blogs, news – essentially, the majority of social media content. And here's where Big Data shines. It can process and interpret this unstructured mayhem with ease.

4.3. The Social Sentiment Analysis

The enormous engagement and sheer ubiquity of social media platforms provide an unfathomably large, real-time dataset. Through Big Data, we can harness this dataset and convert the abstract, subjective world of public sentiment into quantifiable, actionable insights.

How does this transformation occur? The process is popularly called 'sentiment analysis'. A subset of Natural Language Processing (NLP), sentiment analysis involves examining textual data from social media posts and assigning a sentiment score ranging from extremely negative to extremely positive.

This process is like taking the Global digital society's pulse. The sentiment scores, or 'pulse', effectively map the overall social mood concerning various economic events, industries, and even specific companies.

4.4. From Pulse to Prediction: The Role of Pattern Recognition

The big leap in Big Data analytics is a transition from a descriptive model (what is happening) to a predictive model (what is likely to happen). To make this leap, one crucial element we must deal with is pattern identification.

One interesting example is the correlation found between Twitter sentiment scores and the stock market. Upon close inspection, researchers noticed a pattern. Apparently, public sentiments on Twitter could predict stock market movements to a certain extent. The logic makes sense: public emotions often drive buying and selling decisions, affecting stock prices.

4.5. The Power and Pitfall of Social Sentiment Analysis

The potential for Big Data powered sentiment analysis in financial markets is immense. By responding to market sentiment shifts in real-time, investors can make more informed and timely decisions. Institutional investors and hedge funds, with exhaustive resources, are already leveraging this tool for superior market insights and competitive advantage.

However, as with any analysis technique, social sentiment analysis isn't infallible. Challenges such as accurately interpreting sarcastic or misleading posts, the importance of individual influencers, or sudden shifts in public opinion require continuous model refinement and clever algorithm design.

Overall, the advent of Big Data and its marriage with social sentiment has revolutionized our understanding of financial markets. By translating the public opinions and sentiments from social media into quantifiable data, we now have a dynamic, real-time mechanism to monitor the market's pulse. In doing so, we've undoubtedly enriched and diversified the toolset market analysts employ, leading to a more accurate, sensitive, and nuanced understanding of financial markets.

Chapter 5. Algorithmic Trading: The Social Media Fuel

Algorithmic trading has grown significantly in recent years due to advancements in technology, increased computational power and the accessibility of data, including data acquired via social media. These technologies have invigorated trading models that had otherwise been out of reach, thereby, adding an additional layer of complexity to financial market activities. Algorithmic trading uses complex formulas, combined with mathematical models and human oversight, to make decisions about trading stocks and securities.

5.1. Why Algorithms?

The rise of algorithmic trading can be attributed to its multitude of benefits. Algorithms allow traders to execute orders at high speeds, which is beneficial in a fast-paced, constantly fluctuating market. Furthermore, the algorithms are not subjected to emotions and bias, thus they can consistently follow the predetermined trading strategy without deviation. They also eliminate the risk of manual errors in trading and allow users to simultaneously trade multiple accounts or various strategies at one time.

One of the key advantages is the ability to test trading strategies before they are executed in live markets, a process known as backtesting. Through backtesting, traders can assess the viability of their strategy against historical data to ensure its effectiveness before staking real capital.

5.2. Social Media: The New Data Source

The role of social media data in algorithmic trading is a recent yet rapidly evolving phenomenon. Social media platforms, with their millions of user interactions daily, present a goldmine of sentiments and reactions which can provide valuable insights into market trends. Analysis and interpretation of this data are made possible through machine learning models and natural language processing techniques.

Specifically, increasing numbers of algorithmic traders are tapping into the vast array of public information available on social media platforms. This varied data includes real-time news alerts, opinions about specific securities or market conditions, financial reports, articles, and much more. Market sentiments, investment opinions, and even global events breaking on social media can create momentum that impacts market trends.

5.3. From Text to Trading Signal

Creating a successful trading algorithm using social media data goes beyond simply acquiring masses of tweets or Facebook posts. The crux of the challenge lies in the ability to effectively process and interpret this data.

In this regard, Natural Language Processing (NLP) comes into play. NLP is a branch of artificial intelligence that provides machines with the ability to understand, interpret, and generate human language. NLP algorithms classify content based on sentiment (positive, negative, or neutral) and relevance to specific securities or market activities.

The signals derived from the sentiment analysis are then fed into a trading algorithm. This algorithm is programmed with a set of conditions and parameters that dictate when to trade (buy or sell) a target security. When the sentiment signals reach certain thresholds set within these parameters, the algorithm initiates a corresponding action in the trading platform.

5.4. Pitfalls and Contingencies

Despite the vast potential, algorithmic trading using social media data is fraught with significant risks and challenges. The level of noise in social media content is high because not all posts are relevant or accurate. Furthermore, the anonymity of social media allows for the manipulation of market sentiment, thereby leading to false signals. As such, the need for reliable filters and robust data verification methods can't be overstated.

Given these contingencies, algorithmic models should be designed with intrinsic risk management features. This includes placing limits on trade size, frequently monitoring the system's performance, and preparing for unforeseen volatilities by implementing stop-loss measures, among other safeguards.

5.5. The Future: Social Media-Fueled Algorithmic Trading

Despite its inherent challenges, social media fueled algorithmic trading is here to stay and will likely gain more prominence. As technology continues to evolve and become more integrated with financial systems, traders who can harness the power of social media and algorithmic trading are likely to find themselves with an unprecedented competitive advantage.

Nonetheless, it is critical for prospective traders to have a solid understanding of both the technical aspects of algorithmic trading and the role of social media. Practitioners will need to find a balance between automated trading strategies and the ability to interpret the rich qualitative insights found within the conversational tone of social media posts.

To conclude, social media provides a wealth of valuable real-time data for businesses, traders, and investors. We are at the precipice of a significant shift in market operations. Algorithmic trading, fueled by social media, is a vital mechanism in this new financial landscape. The ability to process and analyze large quantities of data from social media platforms could potentially yield significant financial rewards for those able to navigate this complex, yet exciting landscape.

Chapter 6. Machine Learning: The Brain Behind Successful Predictions

Machine Learning forms the backbone of a plethora of prediction algorithms across a multitude of sectors and industries. Financial market prediction, empowered by social media data, is one such field where machine learning algorithms act as the cognitive powerhouse. Therefore, understanding the conceptual intricacies of machine learning and its fundamental role in the realm of predictions in financial markets is indispensable.

6.1. Machine Learning: An Overview

Machine learning is a subset of artificial intelligence, wherein computers are modeled to learn and adapt themselves from the data fed into them, without being programmed explicitly. The systems or models, via learning from the data patterns and making decisions thereof, continue to develop and improve their performance over time. Now, what is interesting to note is that, when we talk about the core concept of machine learning, it is the data, copious amounts of it, that makes all the difference.

6.2. Finance & Social Media Data

As we usher in the era of big data, traditional financial markets no longer solely rely on historical trends and economic indicators. To be more resilient and proactive, financial analysts are now utilizing machine learning to incorporate real-time data from social media to drive their investment strategies and decisions.

In the social media brimming era, data, by its sheer volume, variety, and velocity, is that transformative catalyst. It's here that social media platforms like Twitter, Facebook, and LinkedIn come into play, serving as treasure troves of data, ready to be harnessed for predictive modelling. The data here isn't just enormous but also valuable, encompassing diverse dimensions like user profiles, sentiments, network structures, and the timing of posts which, when analyzed, can generate critical insights.

6.3. Machine Learning at Play

Machine learning and its different techniques play a pivotal role in processing and analyzing this myriad of data. Techniques like Natural Language Processing (NLP) help analyze the textual content, largely unstructured, of social media posts, transforming it into structured datasets. The data can then be mined for sentiments, patterns, and connections that can impact financial markets.

Stream-based machine learning models, owing to the possibility of fluctuating data streams from social media, can handle and learn from such torrential inflow of datapoints, adjusting their prediction formulas accordingly. Machine learning techniques also play a significant role in detecting anomalies, spotting potential manipulations, or identifying critical trend changes in real-time, by continuously monitoring social media data.

6.4. From Data to Predictions: The Machine Learning Process

A multi-faceted process, it begins with data collection, where tweets, posts, and other social media content relevant to specific financial markets or assets are captured. The next step is data preprocessing, involving cleaning, managing, and restructuring of the data to make it suitable for analysis. Techniques like tokenization, stemming, and stop-word removal play key roles in this stage.

Thereafter begins the actual machine learning process, where the preprocessed data is fed into machine learning models. The models are trained and tested iteratively with different sets of data, thereby improving their prediction performance over time. The outcome of this models - the predictions, form the base for investment decisions.

6.5. The Way Ahead

The initial results from integrating machine learning models with social media data have been promising, to say the least. Predictive models equipped with machine learning algorithms significantly perform better in forecasting financial market changes than traditional models. But, the road is still under construction with questions related to data privacy, ethical use of information, and accuracy of predictions that need careful consideration.

In the vast ocean of future finance, where waves of informational currents are generated each minute, machine learning acts as navigational aids for financial analysts. It's the brain which makes social media a viable tool, deeply influencing financial markets predictions.

Chapter 7. Case Studies: The History of Market Movements Influenced by Social Media

In this part of the exploration, we delve deep into a compelling series of chronicles underscoring the profound influence of social media on the ebbs and flows of financial markets. Through a lens that juxtaposes history with finance, we illustrate fascinating cases laying bare the potent interplay between tweets, viral posts, and consequential market shifts.

7.1. The Manic Monday of Facebook's Plummeting Stock

If we rummage through the archives of financial history, we unearth one of the most notable tales of social media's impact on market dynamics - Facebook's dramatic share price plunge in July 2018. Following a gloomy earnings call where the networking giant warned of slow future growth and skyrocketing costs, a dedicated community of investors, influencers, and journalists took to Twitter to disseminate the news, inciting panic that reverberated through markets worldwide. The immediate aftermath saw Facebook's shares going into a free-fall, wiping off over $120 billion off its valuation in just a single trading day. This incident served as a landmark case, emphasizing the might of social media in framing investor sentiments and market trajectories.

7.2. The Short Squeeze Saga: GameStop and Reddit's WallStreetBets

No discourse on social media's influence on the stock market is complete without recounting the extraordinary episode involving GameStop and Reddit's WallStreetBets forum in early 2021. A campaign orchestrated by an army of retail traders on this subreddit fuelled an unforeseen surge in GameStop's stock, causing a 'Short Squeeze' that spelled catastrophe for hedge funds shorting the stock. This extraordinary event initialized a tectonic shift in Wall Street, underscoring the power that collective retail traders could wield when armed with social media, against financial powerhouses. It was a stark demonstration of how social networking platforms could turn established financial frameworks upside down.

7.3. Elon Musk's Tweets and Tesla Stock Volatility

A perpetually trending example of the profound impact of social media posts on stock prices is the curious case of Tesla's CEO, Elon Musk's, interactions on Twitter. Musk's tweets have swung Tesla's stock price multiple times, with casual utterances about potential product developments, financial information, not to mention taking the company private. Particularly infamous was the tweet from August 7, 2018: "Am considering taking Tesla private at $420. Funding secured." This 61-character message sent shockwaves throughout the trading world and led to significant stock price fluctuations. The incident vividly reinforced how a single social media post from a figure of influence could rock market sentiments and stock prices.

7.4. Crypto-craze: Bitcoin, Dogecoin and Social Media Buzz

The nascency of cryptocurrencies has seen the trading landscape bombarded with a unique kind of volatility, largely fueled by social media buzz. Bitcoin's roller-coaster ride, influenced heavily by discussions on platforms like Twitter and Reddit, serves as an apt illustration. Similarly, for the meme-born digital currency, Dogecoin, its price surge was primarily fueled by social media frenzy, oftentimes as a reaction to Elon Musk's tweets supporting it. The matte of cryptocurrencies is still developing, creating an arena where social sentiment holds a pivotal role in dictating market movements.

In essence, these cases form a testament to social media's undeniable significance in modulating financial markets. As we delve further into the 21st century, the intertwining of social media chatter and market trends will only tighten. Recognizing this influence, interpreting it correctly, and integrating it with traditional financial analysis will be the fundamental challenge that modern traders and investors must surmount.

Chapter 8. The Legal Landscape: Ethics, Privacy and Regulation

It is indispensable to delve into the legal and ethical concerns that are intertwined with the amalgamation of social media sentiment in the financial sector. This chapter sheds light on the laws, the regulations governing this intersection, the issues surrounding privacy, and ethical decisions that can come to the forefront.

8.1. The Regulatory Framework

Financial markets worldwide are regulated by strict laws to prevent market manipulation and ensure investor protection. The rise of social media adds another nuance, necessitating these laws to cover the new aspect of market prediction using posts, tweets, and more. In the U.S., for example, the Securities and Exchange Commission (SEC) requires all relevant information about a company to be publicly disseminated. This rule makes it questionable whether tweets and Facebook posts can be used as an official source of company information. The legal landscape is even more intricate when you consider the global nature of social media. Each jurisdiction has its own set of rules on how information can be sourced and disseminated. The financial world, therefore, needs to tread carefully, ensuring that the use of social media sentiment in market predictions does not inadvertently cross any regulatory boundaries.

8.2. Privacy Concerns

Social media is a vast vault of data mined by companies to derive insights and trends. But with this comes the paramount issue of user privacy. A tweet or a Facebook post might feel like shouting into the void, but each of these can add up, forming part of this big data that corporations can access. It begs the question: to what extent is such data collection ethical, and when does it infringe upon an individual's privacy?

Several jurisdictions, such as the European Union, have stringent laws like the General Data Protection Regulation (GDPR) to protect individual privacy, giving individuals the right to know how their data is being used. Organizations, thus, have a responsibility not only to safeguard personal identifiable information (PII) but also to ensure that they are transparent about their data use. For instance, disclosing if they employ it in their algorithmic trading or other financial decision-making processes.

8.3. Ethical Considerations

Alongside legal and privacy issues, ethical considerations can be equally significant in this arena. The question arises, is it morally right to use an individual's social media sentiment, however public it might be, to forecast market trends or drive financial decisions? This question becomes murkier given the potential power of social media to manipulate sentiments, a point underscored by the controversies around 'fake news' and its impact on economic factors.

Moreover, ethical considerations extend to the possible exclusion of certain investor groups. Those without social media presence or the knowledge to leverage it might find themselves at an unfair disadvantage.

8.4. Navigating the Terrain

Given these intricacies, financial institutions, investors, and regulators must come together to navigate this evolving landscape. A combined approach, where the power of social media insights is harnessed following strict legal, privacy, and ethical parameters, is necessary. This includes creating protocols for data handling and decision-making based on social media sentiments, setting up bodies to track any misleading information, and ensuring transparency.

Within these discussions, one must also consider establishing an international regulatory body given the global nature of both financial markets and social media. This would help set guidelines that transcend national boundaries while balancing the potential advantages of using social media with privacy concerns, ethics, and laws.

To conclude, the integration of social media sentiment with financial markets is an exciting new frontier with seemingly endless possibilities. By recognizing the inherent legal, privacy, and ethical implications, the financial world can ensure this exploration is responsible, inclusive, and fair, setting the stage for a groundbreaking approach to predicting market trends.

Chapter 9. Modern Investor: Adapting to a Socially-Informed Market

The contemporary investor is stepping into a new era, one that is being remodeled and dictated by the pervasive influence of social media. As the financial market landscape undergoes this progressive shift towards a more socially-informed outlook, it is vital that an investor adapts and embraces these changes. Investors of today must gear up for this paradigm shift, learning to incorporate social media into their investment strategies, to dissect and interpret big data, and to recognize the value and implications of social sentiment in market fluctuations.

9.1. Harnessing the Power of Social Media

The first leg of this transformative journey entails acknowledging the massive wealth of information that social media platforms are constantly generating. These platforms, armed with millions of users globally, function as sizable data mines capturing a real-time pulse of public sentiment. Recognizing these platforms' potential can significantly augment an investor's knowledge base, enhancing their strategic decision-making capabilities.

Information circulating on social media is often immediate, offering investors a live snapshot of current market sentiment. Investors can scrutinize these vast information troves for patterns related to specific securities or the market as a whole.

9.2. Understanding Big Data

Social media platforms generate an astronomical volume of information every second. Referred to as Big Data, this colossal information resource can significantly aid investment strategies. From tweets to Facebook posts, every bit of information forms part of this Big Data.

With the right tools and analysis, this vast, unstructured data can be transformed into valuable insights. The trend prediction capabilities of Big Data, coupled with machine learning algorithms, can enable investors to generate potentially profitable trading signals. Therefore, understanding and decoding Big Data can prove instrumental in enhancing an investor's market acumen.

9.3. Grasping Social Sentiment

At its core, every market movement has a kernel of human sentiment. Social sentiment refers to the collective attitude of social media users towards any given topic at any given time. As the attitudes change, social sentiment fluctuates.

These fluctuations, when measured accurately, can provide investors with a laboratory of human behavioral study. An investor who comprehends how social sentiment influences market trends stands to gain an edge over those unacquainted with this perspective. It's valuable to learn how to measure and interpret social sentiment to predict market movements accurately.

9.4. Leveraging Algorithmic Trading

With social media platforms producing data every moment, processing it manually becomes unfeasible. Here comes the role of algorithmic trading. It uses sophisticated algorithms that can comb through this data, identify patterns, and make trading decisions.

This approach broadens the scope of an investor's capabilities by providing quantitative trading solutions based on analyzed social media data. Subsequently, one doesn't have to be an expert programmer to employ algorithmic trading. Many companies are providing simplistic and user-friendly algorithmic trading solutions.

9.5. Navigating the Legal Landscape

Remember that with any new technology comes a new territory of legal and ethical concerns. Therefore, investing based on information sourced from social media must be carried out judiciously. It's paramount for investors to stay informed about regulatory changes related to exploiting social media data. Following guidelines and maintaining ethical boundaries enhances an investor's credibility in the market.

9.6. Practical Case Studies

Incorporating real-world case studies into one's learning journey grants a practical edge. Observing how social media influenced certain market movements and the consequences thereof presents investors with valuable lessons. It showcases how theory translates into practice and the potential pitfalls to be wary of.

As we look ahead, it is becoming increasingly clear that the contemporary investor's role must evolve in tandem with technological progress. By actively seeking knowledge and understanding the impact of these digital trends on market predictions, investors can position themselves well in this rapidly shifting ecosystem. The age of the modern investor acknowledges the power and potential of social media as a game-changing tool for financial decision-making. Thus, it becomes crucial for investors to adapt and thrive in this digitally pervasive age, pivoting habits and usual practices to harness the boons of a socially-informed market.

Chapter 10. Forecasting the Future: Predictive Trends and Models

The endless march of time carries with it the forward propagation of financial markets and social media trends, constantly modifying the digital terrain. In an effort to leverage the power of combined financial and social data, predictive modeling has emerged as an incontrovertible tool. With the aid of such models, market participants aim to forecast future events based on present conditions and past historical data to ultimately make lucrative investment decisions.

10.1. Big Data and Predictive Modeling

In the context of predictive modeling, big data merely refers to an all-inclusive set of data that is too large or complex to be handled by traditional data-processing software. This landscape is characterized by the 'three Vs' — volume, velocity, and variety. Amid these complex attributes, it hides nuggets of valuable insights waiting to be discovered and parsed by trained analysts.

The data assortment from social media platforms, financial markets, and additional sources is a treasure trove of information which machine learning algorithms can mine for correlations, trends, and potentially profitable insights. These data points, like tweets or comments, holdings, and sector trends, hybridize into a complex data fabric that forms the foundation for developing predictive models.

10.2. The Invincibles: Machine Learning Predictive Models

Machine learning predictive models swing into action here as the mighty conquerors of this data deluge. They sift through immense quantities, examining various correlations, finding subtle patterns, and marking noteworthy trends.

Machine learning algorithms employ different techniques, including linear regression, decision tree analysis, and neural networks to extract patterns and make predictions. Models like gradient boosting decision trees, recurrent neural networks (RNNs), and long short-term memory (LSTM) networks, each with their unique strengths, are particularly beneficial in forecasting the stock market's future behavior through harnessing social media sentiments.

For instance, LSTM, a recurrent neural network architecture, works exceptionally well with time-series data by remembering long-term patterns, something that traditional RNNs struggled with. This particular feature makes LSTM networks ideally suited for analyzing financial markets, which are influenced by a multitude of factors over time.

10.3. Real World Model Implementations

In reality, several firms have started utilizing predictive models and machine learning to forecast the financial markets. Predictive analytics startup, Predata, uses signals from social and collaborative media to forecast political events that might affect financial outcomes. Similarly, Eagle Alpha leverages its Digital Insights product to extract predictive signals from social media to better understand consumer trends, earnings predictions, and macro indicators.

Additionally, research papers bearing titles such as 'Twitter mood predicts the stock market,' offer profound testament to the rising influence of social media sentiment on financial markets' behavior, thereby validating the efficacy of predictive models in the financial domain.

10.4. Predictions: A Combination of Art and Science

While the technical process of creating predictive models may seem purely scientific, there exists a subtle yet decisive artistry in determining how to interpret and use the outcomes. Not all patterns are meaningful, not all correlations are causal, and the noise can often overpower the signal. Therefore, a key aspect of predictive modeling involves understanding which potential leads to follow and which to ignore.

10.5. Ethical Considerations and Regulatory Challenges

While immense potential lies in predictive models leveraged for financial market forecasting, ethical and regulatory hurdles cannot be ignored. Data privacy regulations, like the General Data Protection Regulation (GDPR), govern data aggregation and usage, shaping how predictive analytics can be employed. Ethical considerations concerning predatory and manipulative practices also need to be addressed. An appropriate balance where both innovation and regulation flourish in harmony must be sought to ensure a fair and just market ecosystem.

10.6. The Road Ahead

As we unravel potential predictive patterns and trends in worldwide financial markets, we stand at the tipping point between knowledge and wisdom, data and insight. The successful navigation of this path hinges on gaining a profound understanding of the capabilities and limitations of predictive models, and using them in a way that is profitable, ethical, and responsible.

The future is poised to see a further deepening of the integration of social media sentiment analysis, predictive modeling, machine learning, and financial markets. This intersection promises not only novel insights and potentially lucrative predictions but also significant challenges that we must address head-on. As we venture into this brave new world, it is clear that the future is here - it's just not evenly distributed.

Chapter 11. Social Media Investing: The New Norm and Best Practices

In our contemporary digital era, social media landscape has been transformed from a simple networking platform to a sophisticated hub of information, impacting every sphere of human activity - including the financial market. The emerging field of social media investing has revolutionized traditional investing norms, ushering a new era of social connectivity for investors, traders, and brokers alike. This chapter meticulously examines this new norm of social media investing and explores various practical guidelines for its most effective utilization.

11.1. The Underpinnings of Social Media Investing

Social media investing refers to the practice of employing social media channels to glean insights and trends that can be used to guide investment decisions. Financial market participants engage in continuous monitoring of various social platforms like Twitter, Facebook, LinkedIn, and even Reddit to tap the pulse of the social populace. The perception of this pulse, the sentiment of the crowd, holds the potential to influence the stock markets.

This transformation in investing strategies has been driven by two interconnected trends - exponential increase in social media usage and the rapid growth of big data technology. With the former providing a wealth of data for the latter to analyze, the integration of these two trends has been the catalyst for a new form of transactional analysis.

Analysts pour over millions of posts, comments, likes, shares, and tweets, feeding this unstructured data into sophisticated machine learning algorithms capable of discerning sentiment, trend, and buzz. This discernment guides decisions about buying, selling, and holding stocks.

11.2. Best Practices for Social Media Investing

While social media investing has unfolded a new horizon for investment strategies, it demands prudent and responsible usage. To ensure the effective implementation of this investment methodology, the following best practices are prominent.

1. **Diversify Your Sources:** Avoid solely depending on a single social platform, as user demographics and behavior can vary. Diversify by monitoring various social channels and professional trading networks.

2. **Use Advanced Tools:** Leverage big data and machine learning tools to automate the sentiment analysis process. Sophisticated tools like R, Python, sentiment analysis APIs are available to perform large scale predictive analysis accurately.

3. **Stay Updated:** Technology and social media trends evolve rapidly. Continuous learning and staying abreast of the latest trends is vital to capture the maximum returns.

4. **Integrate Both Quantitative and Qualitative Analysis:** Algorithmic analysis is critical, but human interpretation of wider market factors remains important. Use the power of social media investing to supplement not to supplant traditional analysis methods.

5. **Remain Ethical and Legal:** Always respect privacy rules and other legal regulations when collecting and analyzing social media data. Ethical conduct ensures trust and long-term success.

11.3. The Implications and Future Trends of Social Media Investing

The emergence of social media investing not only signifies the transformative power of digital technologies, but also indicates larger cultural shifts towards transparency and social decision-making. The democratization of financial information that once was exclusive to Wall Street has had profound implications on financial markets and investment strategies.

As for the future, we expect to see new methods of collecting and analyzing social data, an acceleration in the use of machine learning for predictive modeling, and a greater emphasis on real-time sentiment analysis. Additionally, privacy concerns, regulatory influences on social media, and the potential for social platform-created investment tools also present interesting areas for future observation.

In conclusion, social media investing has fundamentally altered how we make investment decisions. However, as with any powerful tool, it demands knowledge, sophistication, and ethical diligence for its effective and responsible use. Social media has transformed from a networking platform to a forecasting tool, a bridge that connects the reality of the stock market with the sentiment of the people. And while it is not a utopian solution for market predictions, it does represent a significant breakthrough in leveraging digital trends for financial decisions. As we look towards a future where the physical and digital realms increasingly intertwine, investors who master this new norm and its best practices will remain ahead of the curve, prepared to thrive in an ever-evolving marketplace.

www.ingramcontent.com/pod-product-compliance
Lightning Source LLC
Chambersburg PA
CBHW060900260726
48661CB00008B/3364